DISCOVERING GEOGRAPHY

CITIES AND TOWNS

FRAN SAMMIS

ART BY RICHARD MACCABE

BENCHMARK BOOKS

MARSHALL CAVENDISH

NEW YORK

Benchmark Books
Marshall Cavendish Corporation
99 White Plains Road
Tarrytown, New York 10591

©Marshall Cavendish Corporation, 1998

Series created by Blackbirch Graphics, Inc.

Printed and bound in the United States.

Library of Congress Cataloging-in-Publication Data

Sammis, Fran.
    Cities and towns / by Fran Sammis.
        p.   cm. — (Discovering geography)
    Includes index.
    Summary: Text, maps, and activities help the reader explore various aspects of cities and towns.
    ISBN 0-7614-0540-2 (lib. bdg.)
    1. Cities and towns—Juvenile literature. [1. Cities and towns. 2. Maps.] I. Title. II. Series: Discovering geography (New York, N.Y.)
HT119.S25   1998
307.76—dc21
                                                                    97-322
                                                                       CIP
                                                                        AC

Contents

Color It Green   4

What's New at the Zoo?   6

Paper Route   8

East Side, West Side   10

Turn Right at the Light   12

Plan a Parade   14

Where Is the Video Store?   16

Stop Here, Please   18

Taxi!   20

Meet Me at the Mummy   22

You Are Here   24

Make Your Own Map   26

Answers   28

Glossary   31

Index   32

Color It Green

Color is one of the things mapmakers use to make maps easier to read. Copy or trace the map on the next page. Then, color your map according to the key below. See how much easier it is to spot things that are the same when they are in color.

KEY

CORN FIELD	HOUSE
PLOWED FIELD	BARN
GRASS/PRAIRIE	STORE/OFFICE
FOREST	FOX RIVER PRINCE POND
APPLE ORCHARD	ROAD

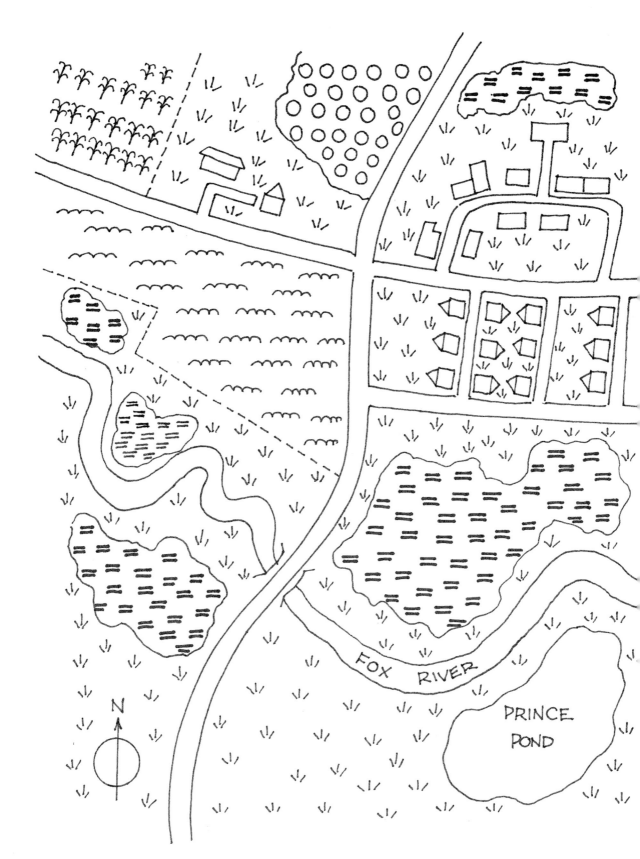

N

FOX RIVER

PRINCE
POND

What's New at the Zoo?

Symbols are used on a map to keep it neat and easy to read. They also make a map more interesting. Some of the symbols for the zoo map on the next page are identified below. Some you will have to guess at.

- How many Information Booths are there? Where are they?

- Where are the restrooms?

- Go in the North Gate and head for the nearest snack bar. Which animals will you pass?

- Is Flamingo Lake north or south of Monkey Island?

- Go north from the restaurant and turn left at the first path. What animals are on your left as you walk to the fountain?

- Is the Bird House closer to the Gift Shop or the lions?

- Take the outside path around the zoo. Which animals do you see?

Symbols have to be drawn much more simply than the things they represent.

Paper Route

You can use maps to help you do all kinds of things, like deliver papers to earn extra money. Start your own paper route! Grab your bike, a map, and paper and pencil to keep track of your customers' addresses. Start from your house.

- Your first customer lives in the 500 block of Maple. It's the third house with an even-numbered address.

- Next turn north on Main St. Skip the first odd-numbered house, deliver to all the other odd-numbered houses.

- At Elm St., turn around and head back south. Deliver to the second even-numbered house in the 4500 block.

- Take Willow to Burlington, go north to Maple. Turn left. Leave a paper at the house on the south side of the street that should have the higher-numbered address. What number should the address begin with?

- Drop a paper at Mrs. Smith's house. Does she have an odd- or even-numbered address?

- Go north on Curtiss to Elm St. Turn east. Go to 1st St. and head south to the Browns. What number should their address begin with? Should their address be larger or smaller than their next door neighbor's?

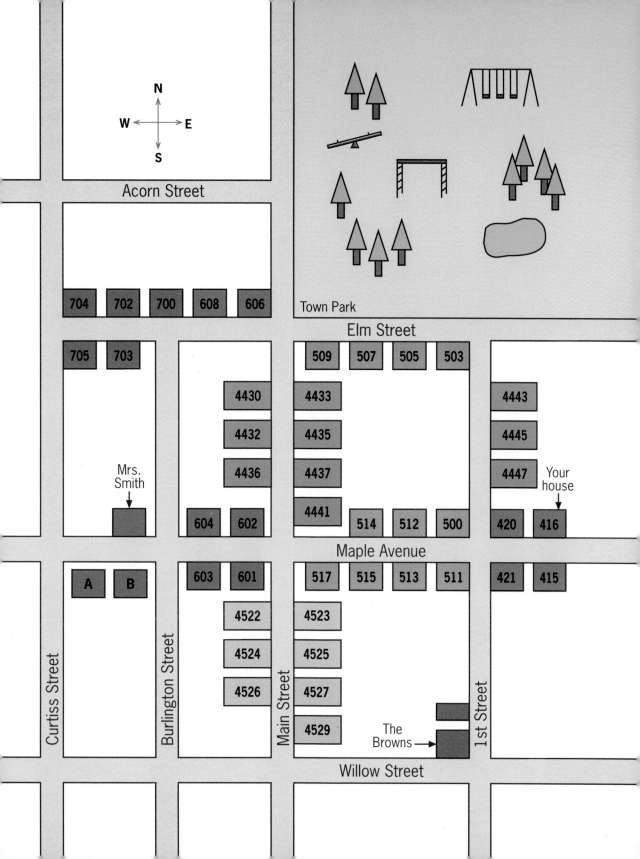

East Side, West Side

Play this game with a friend. You will need paper and pencil, coins or buttons for markers, one of a pair of dice, and six same-size pieces of paper. Mark the papers from A to F.

Main Street divides this town into an East Side and a West Side. Choose a side. Then, write down six of the places that are located on your side of town. (The playground and parking lot count as places.)

Grid coordinates like these tell you where something is on a map.

Place the letters in a paper cup. Draw a letter out, then roll the die. Call out the combination, such as A2 or D5, for example. If the sector (section) contains a place that is on a player's list, that player puts a marker on it.

Put the letter back in the cup, shake it up, then draw and roll again (take turns). The first player to cover all the places on his or her list is the winner.

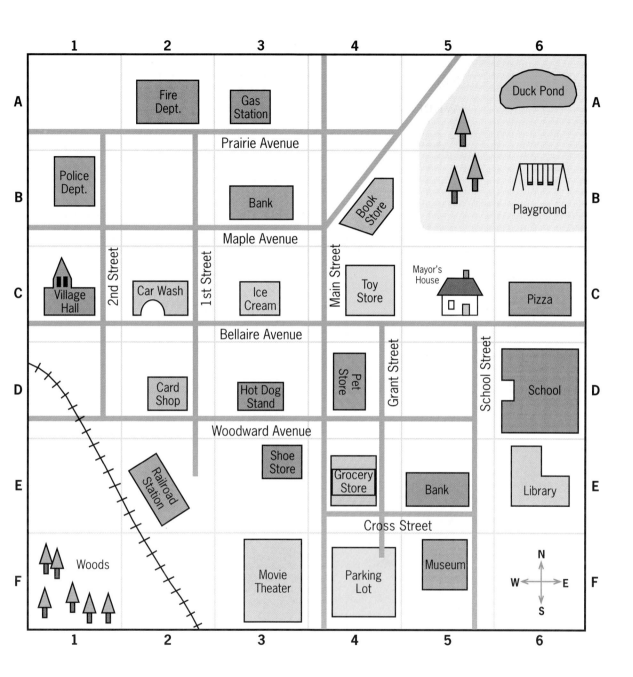

Turn Right at the Light

Use the map, follow the directions, and see where you end up!

- Leave school by the Pierce Street door. Turn left and go to the light, turn right, and go to the third store on your right. What can you buy?

- You're meeting a friend on the northeast corner of Wood Ave. and Main St. What's on that corner?

- You're at the parking lot. Exit and head west. Go to the end of the block and turn right. Go one block and turn right again! Go to the first stoplight. Where are you?

- Who lives in the second house south of the light on the east side of Wilson Ave.?

Mrs. Johnson lives in the apartments on Wood Ave. You walk her dog, Chief, for her.

- Go south to Park St. Turn left. What direction are you heading?

- You and Chief then stop at the second house on the left. Who are you visiting?

- The three of you then jog up Wilson Ave. to the park. How many blocks do you jog?

Now, make up your own directions and challenge a friend to follow them.

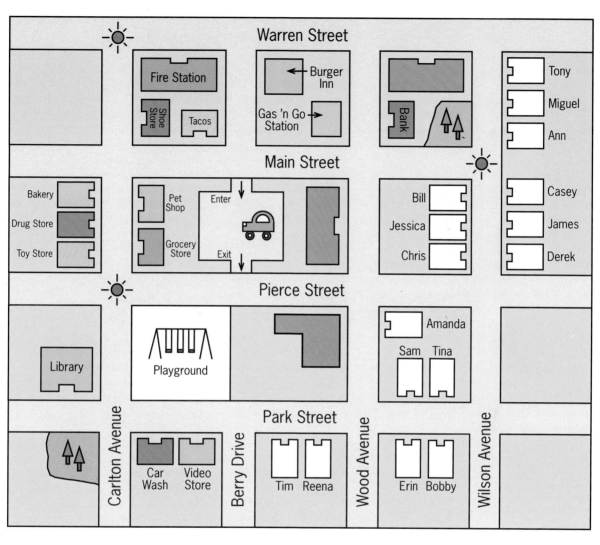

Warren Street

Fire Station
Shoe Store
Tacos

Burger Inn
Gas 'n Go Station

Bank

Tony
Miguel
Ann

Main Street

Bakery
Drug Store
Toy Store

Pet Shop
Grocery Store
Enter
Exit

Bill
Jessica
Chris

Casey
James
Derek

Pierce Street

Library

Playground

Amanda
Sam   Tina

Park Street

Car Wash
Video Store

Tim   Reena

Erin   Bobby

Carlton Avenue
Berry Drive
Wood Avenue
Wilson Avenue

N
W   E
S

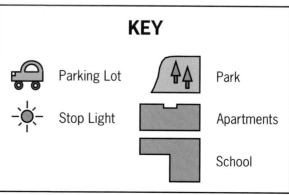

KEY

Parking Lot

Stop Light

Park

Apartments

School

Plan a Parade

You're in charge of the Fourth of July parade. The parade will start at the City Parking Lot and end at Arrowhead Park. Use the key below to help you read the map. You will need to direct the parade on a long route past:

- the office building on Cherokee
- all the stores on South Main Street
- the library and the school
- all the houses on North Main Street
- the bank on Elm Place

If you were in a hurry, what would be the shortest route from the City Lot to Arrowhead Park? Be careful! The lines at the car wash on 1st Avenue always block traffic, and the parade can't go by the hospital—it's in a Quiet Zone.

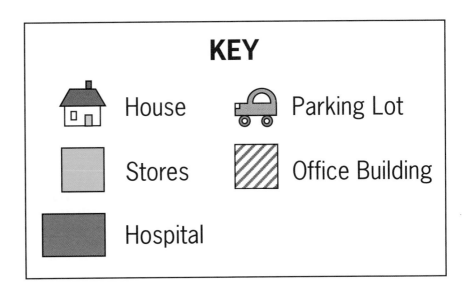

KEY

House   Parking Lot

Stores   Office Building

Hospital

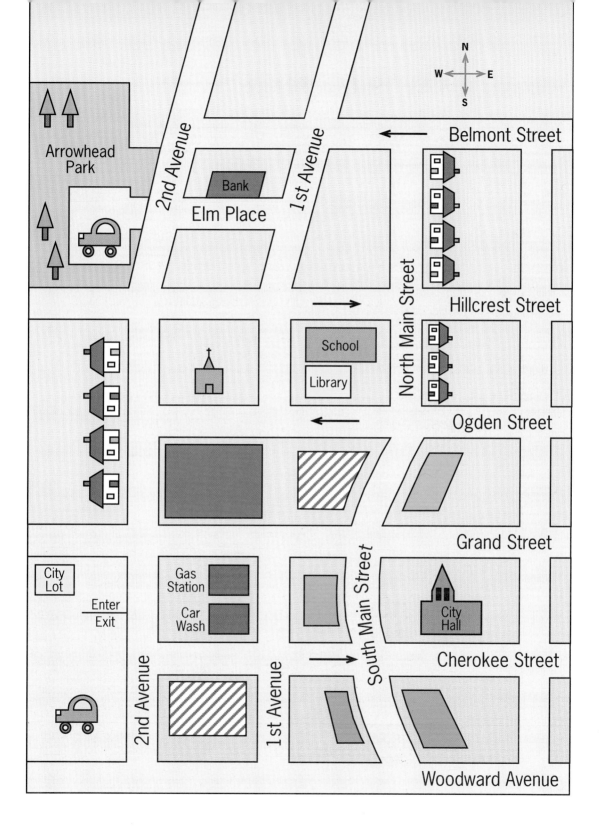

Where Is the Video Store?

Whoops! The mapmaker forgot to finish the map on the next page. Copy or trace the map, then use the directions and symbols below to complete it.

- The southwest corner of town is a park. There is a parking lot where the hiking trail begins. There is a duck pond in the southeast corner of the park.

- There is a house on the east side of Mill Court. There are 5 houses on the north side of Adams. (Three out of the five houses are west of Market Street.)

- Two intersections have stop lights: Maple and Lincoln, and Washington and Elm.

- The pet shop is on the north side of Lincoln Avenue at Market Street. The video store is on Lincoln Avenue across from the pet shop. There is a restaurant south of the video store.

- A school is on the northeast corner of Washington and Elm.

- There are woods on the east side of Pine Road between Washington Avenue and Lincoln Avenue.

- There are 3 office buildings on the east side of Market Street, south of Cross Street.

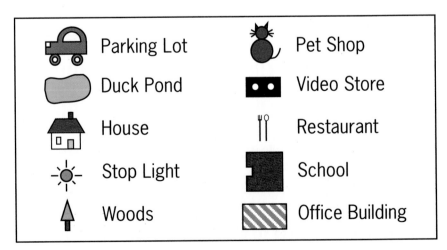

Parking Lot		Pet Shop	
Duck Pond		Video Store	
House		Restaurant	
Stop Light		School	
Woods		Office Building	

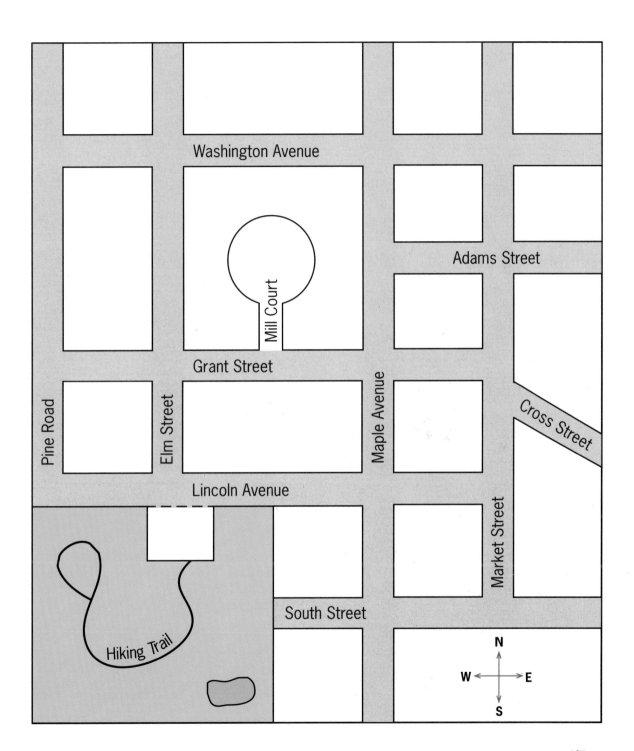

Washington Avenue

Mill Court

Adams Street

Grant Street

Pine Road

Elm Street

Maple Avenue

Cross Street

Lincoln Avenue

Market Street

Hiking Trail

South Street

N
W ← → E
S

Stop Here, Please

Use this bus map to plan some trips around the city. You might stay on one bus for a whole trip, or you might have to change buses.

- You catch the #42 bus at Canal Street and get off at the fourth stop without changing buses. Where are you?

- How would you get to the Football Stadium if you catch the #20 bus at North Avenue?

- You're at Madison Street. How would you get to the Main Library? To Symphony Hall? To the Pier?

- You catch the bus at Field Road. How would you get to Blackwell Forest Preserve? How many stops away is it?

- There's a good movie at a theater on Ohio Street. If you catch the #42 bus at Dearborn Street, what are two ways you can get to the theater?

A linear map doesn't try to show what a place really looks like.

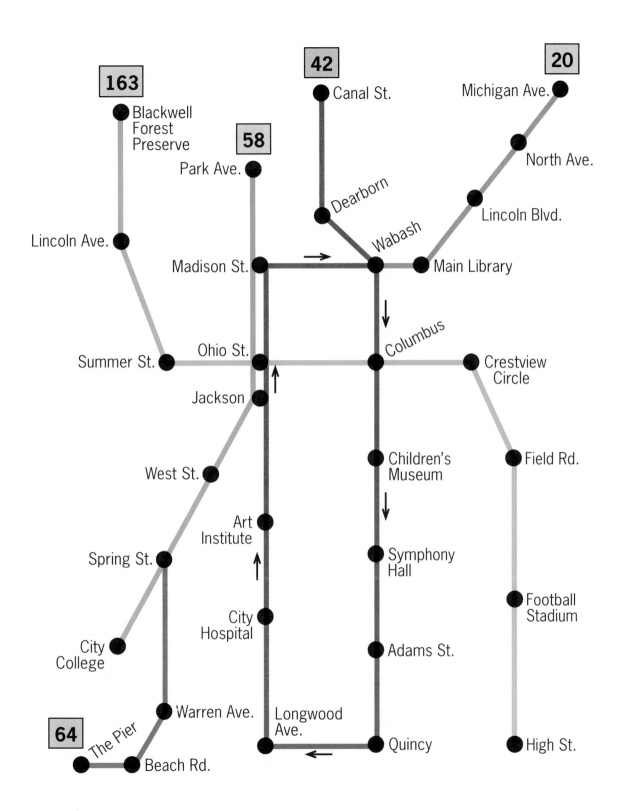

Taxi!

A taxicab ride costs 50 cents a block. How much would the fare be from:

- your house (A) to your grandmother's apartment (B) if you take Warren Ave. to Pierce St.?

- your house to your grandmother's if you stop at the Pizza Palace (C) first to pick up a pepperoni pizza?

- If no one takes a detour, who pays less to get to the Pizza Palace: you (A) or your friend (E)?

- Your grandmother wants to go from her apartment (B) to the grocery store (D) and the bakery (F). Which route costs more: taking School St. to Lake St. to stop at the grocery store first; or taking Pierce St. to Dune Rd. to stop at the bakery first?

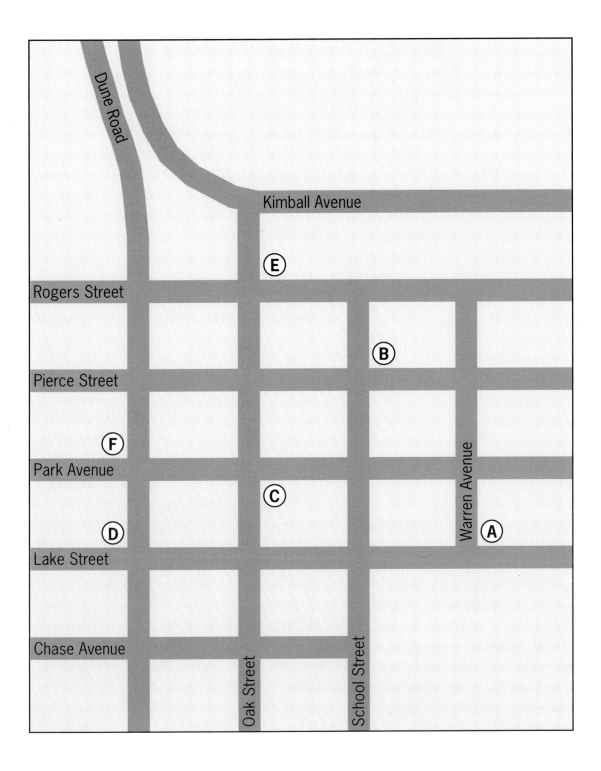

Meet Me at the Mummy

It's field trip time! Unfortunately, the new Natural History Museum maps aren't quite finished. But you can explore anyway. Choose a tour and write down the numbers of your stops. See if you went to the right places.

Tour 1: Stop first at the Information Desk. Then go to the Australia, Oceans, Insects, and Indians exhibits. Your stomach is growling. Visit the Restaurant. Eat fast—your teacher wants a report on the Woodlands. Uh oh! The bus has a flat tire. Find the phone and call home to say you'll be late.

Tour 2: Head straight for the Fossils. Next up: Butterflies, the Hands-On area, and the Gems and Minerals exhibit. You brought your lunch, so you eat in the Picnic Room. It's nice—no ants! Check out the ancient Egypt exhibit, then stop at the Gift Shop to get postcards of the mummies. Finish up with a look at the Dinosaurs.

After you take both tours, make up one of your own and challenge a friend to try it out.

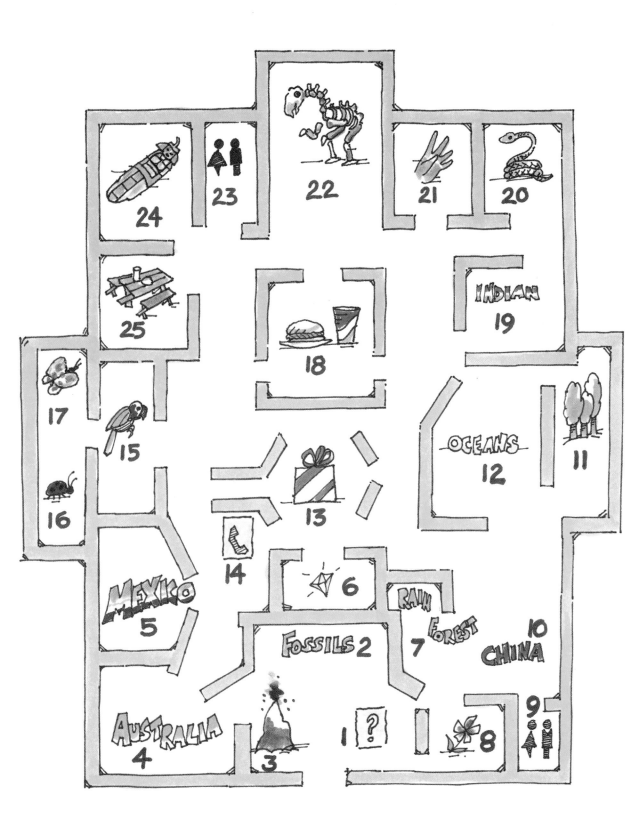

24

23

22

21

20

25

19

17

18

OCEANS
12

11

15

16

13

14

MEXICO
5

6

RAIN
FOREST

CHINA
10

FOSSILS 2

7

9

1

?

8

AUSTRALIA
4

3

You Are Here

It's a gray, rainy day—perfect for cruising the mall. Use the Directory and map to help you get around.

- You need new basketball shoes and jeans, and your favorite movie is now on video. Which three stores will you head for? Which one are you closest to right now? Where would you go next? Is an escalator or elevator closer to your last stop?

- Your best friend loves to eat. How many food places are on the Lower Level? How many on the Upper Level? Which is farthest from where you are? What store is across from it?

DIRECTORY

CLOTHES
K.C. Taylor
125 T-Tops
126 Just Jeans
129 Oh Baby!
219 The Coat Closet

FOOD
Food Court
133 Cookies #1
208 Cookies #2
214 Sweet Tooth Candy

MUSIC/ENTERTAINMENT
127 Music & Video
209 The Music Box

SHOES
K.C. Taylor
123 His and Hers
124 Little Feet
211 The Sporty Foot

SPECIALTY SHOPS
131 Candlelight
203 Card Shop
213 Coffee Beans

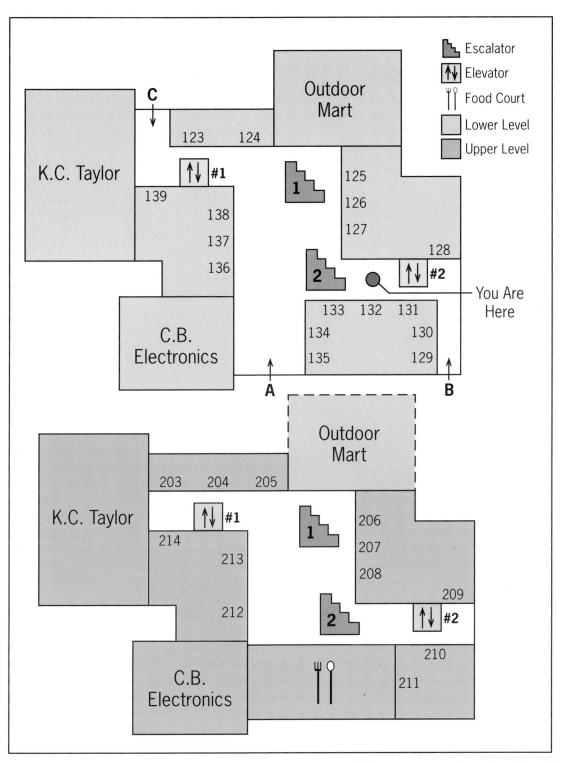

Escalator
Elevator
Food Court
Lower Level
Upper Level

Outdoor Mart

C
123 124
125 126 127 128
#1 1
139
138 137 136
2
#2
You Are Here
133 132 131
134 130
135 129
A B
C.B. Electronics
K.C. Taylor

Outdoor Mart

203 204 205
206 207 208
#1 1
214
213
212
2
#2 209
210 211
C.B. Electronics
K.C. Taylor

Billings County Public School Dist. No. 1
Box 307
Medora, North Dakota 58045

Make Your Own Map

Map your neighborhood or some other part of town you know well. Think up symbols that will be easy to interpret. Color code some areas. Challenge your friends or family to identify the different places or things on your map. Or, see if they can use the map to get from one place to another. If they have problems with your map, find out why. Then, see if you can make another map that is easier to use.

Remember to use a compass symbol.

Here is an example of a key and a neighborhood map.

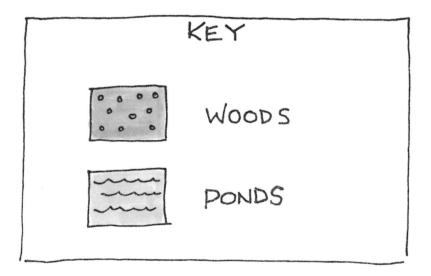

Answers

Pps. 4–5, Color It Green

No answers.

Pps. 6–7, What's New at the Zoo?

There are two Information Booths; one by the North Gate and one by the Gift Shop.

There are restrooms near the North Gate, the South Gate, the kangaroos, and in the Children's Zoo.

If you head for the nearest snack bar after you enter the North Gate, you will pass by the lions and tigers.

Flamingo Lake is south of Monkey Island.

You will see giraffes, elephants, and camels on your way from the restaurant to the fountain.

The Bird House is closer to the Gift Shop than the lions.

Taking the outside path around the zoo, you will see birds, flamingos, kangaroos, camels, snakes, tigers, lions, and bears.

Pps. 8–9, Paper Route

514

4437, 4435, 4433

4524

House A (because the numbers get larger as you go west), and the address will begin with a 7 because this is the 700 block.

Since the even-numbered addresses are on the north side of the east-west streets, Mrs. Smith's house number will be an even number.

The Browns' address will begin with a 4 because they are in the 4500 block of 1st Street, and it will be larger than their next door neighbor's address because the numbers get larger as you go south.

Pps. 10–11, East Side, West Side

No answers.

Pps. 12–13, Turn Right at the Light

You will be at the shoe store, so you can buy those new shoes you wanted.

The bank is your meeting place.

You're at Wilson Avenue.

James lives there.

When you make that first turn with Chief, you'll be headed east.

The two of you stop to visit Tina.

The three of you jog two blocks up Wilson Avenue to reach the park.

Pps. 14–15, Plan a Parade

The trickiest part of the long parade route is figuring out how to march past all the houses on North Main Street. There are a couple of ways to do it. This shows one way. It also shows the shortest route to the park.

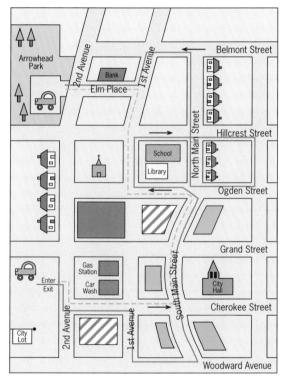

—— Long Route

- - - Short Route

Pps. 16–17, Where Is the Video Store?

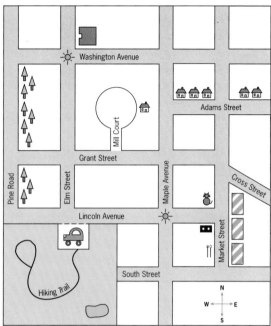

Pps. 18–19, Stop Here, Please

The Children's Museum.

You'd take the #20 bus to Wabash, change to the #42 bus and go to Columbus, then change to the #163 bus and take that one to the Football Stadium.

You'd take the #42 bus to Wabash, then the #20 bus to the Main Library. You'd take the #42 bus all the way to Symphony Hall. You'd take the #58 bus to Spring Street, then catch the #64 bus to the Pier.

You'd stay on the #163 bus all the way from Field Road to Blackwell Forest Preserve, which is six stops away.

You can change to the #163 bus at Columbus, or you can stay on the #42 all the way down and around to its stop at Ohio Street.

Pps. 20-21, Taxi!

$1.50 (3 blocks x 50 cents)

$2.50 (5 blocks x 50 cents)

It will cost more for you to take a taxi to the Pizza Palace (3 blocks x 50 cents = $1.50) than for your friend to go there (2 blocks x 50 cents = $1.00)

It will cost more for your grandmother to stop at the grocery store first (4 blocks x 50 cents = $2.00) than the bakery first (3 blocks x 50 cents = $1.50)

Pps. 22-23, Meet Me at the Mummy

Tour 1: 1, 4, 12, 16, 19, 18, 11, 14

Tour 2: 2, 17, 21, 6, 25, 24, 13, 22

Pps. 24-25, You Are Here

There are several stores you might go to, but your best bets are probably The Sporty Foot (211), Just Jeans (126), and Music & Video (127). You're closest to number 127, so you pick up the video first. Stop next door for the jeans, then take elevator #2 to the second level to get your basketball shoes.

Your best friend won't want to stick around the Lower Level for long—there's only one food place: Cookies #1 (133). The Upper Level has three: Cookies #2 (208), Sweet Tooth Candy (214) and—best of all!—the Food Court. Sweet Tooth Candy is the farthest from where you are right now, and the Card Shop (203) is across from it.

Pps. 26–27, Make Your Own Map

No answers.

Glossary

coordinates A letter and number combination that locates a specific section of a grid.

even-numbered address An address number that ends in 0, 2, 4, 6, or 8.

grid Lines that divide a map into equal-sized squares. Grids help map readers to easily locate points.

intersection The point at which two or more things, such as streets, meet or cross.

key A list that explains the codes used on a map. The key is sometimes called the legend.

legend Another name for the map key.

linear map A route map drawn with straight lines and, often, with all points on the route spaced evenly apart. This makes the map very simple to read. Bus and subway maps are examples of linear maps.

odd-numbered address An address number that ends in 1, 3, 5, 7, or 9.

sector Section. Grid lines divide maps into sectors. Streets divide cities and towns into sectors that are referred to by compass points. For example, the east side, north side, or southwest corner.

symbol A drawing or color that stands for a feature appearing on a map. Symbols help keep maps uncluttered so they are easier to read. Symbols also make maps look more interesting.

Index

B

bus map, 18–19

C

color code, 4, 26
compass symbol, 26

D

directory, 24

E

even-number addresses, 8

G

grid coordinates, 10

I

intersections, 16

K

key, 4, 13, 14, 26

L

linear map, 18

M

mall map, 25
mapmakers, 4, 16
museum map, 22–23

N

neighborhood map, 26–27

O

odd-numbered addresses, 8

P

paper route map, 8–9
parade route map, 14–15

R

routes, 14, 18, 20

S

sector, 10
symbols, 6, 16

Z

zoo map, 6–7